WELCOME TO THE U.S.A.
NEW HAMPSHIRE

Written by Ann Heinrichs Illustrated by Matt Kania
Content Adviser: Ann Hoey, Children's Coordinator, New Hampshire
State Library, Concord, New Hampshire

The Child's World

(handwritten) 917.42 Heinrichs

Published in the United States of America by The Child's World®
PO Box 326 • Chanhassen, MN 55317-0326
800-599-READ • www.childsworld.com

Photo Credits
Cover: Getty Images/Stone/Robert Bossi; frontispiece: Getty Images/Stone/Siegfried Layda.

Interior: AP/Wide World Photo/Jim Cole: 29, 34; AP/Wide World Photo/Joseph Mehling: 33; Corbis: 13 (Bob Krist), 17 (Lee Snider/Photo Images), 25 (Robert Holmes), 30 (Joseph Sohm/ChromoSohm Inc.); Getty Images/Stone/Robert Bossi: 6; Hampshire Pewter Company: 21; Hampton Beach Seafood Festival: 9; Lori Healy/Squam Lakes Natural Science Center, Holderness, NH: 10; Manchester Historic Association: 18; Mount Kearsarge Indian Museum: 14; Don Sykes/Friendly Farm: 26; Waterville Valley Celtic Festival: 22.

Acknowledgments
The Child's World®: Mary Berendes, Publishing Director

Editorial Directions, Inc.: Editorial Directions, Inc.: E. Russell Primm, Editorial Director; Katie Marsico, Associate Editor; Judith Shiffer, Assistant Editor; Matt Messbarger, Editorial Assistant; Susan Hindman, Copy Editor; Melissa McDaniel, Proofreader; Kevin Cunningham, Peter Garnham, Matt Messbarger, Olivia Nellums, Chris Simms, Molly Symmonds, Katherine Trickle, Carl Stephen Wender, Fact Checkers; Tim Griffin/IndexServ, Indexer; Cian Loughlin O'Day, Photo Researcher and Editor

The Design Lab: Kathleen Petelinsek, Design; Julia Goozen, Art Production

Library of Congress Cataloging-in-Publication Data
Heinrichs, Ann.
    New Hampshire / by Ann Heinrichs ; cartography and illustrations by Matt Kania.
        p. cm. — (Welcome to the U.S.A.)
    Includes bibliographical references and index.
    ISBN 1-59296-477-X (library bound : alk. paper)
    1. New Hampshire—Juvenile literature. I. Kania, Matt, ill. II. Title.
F34.3H455 2005
974.2—dc22   2005015055

Ann Heinrichs is the author of more than 100 books for children and young adults. She has also enjoyed successful careers as a children's book editor and an advertising copywriter. Ann grew up in Fort Smith, Arkansas, and lives in Chicago, Illinois.

About the Author
Ann Heinrichs

Matt Kania loves maps and, as a kid, dreamed of making them. In school he studied geography and cartography, and today he makes maps for a living. Matt's favorite thing about drawing maps is learning about the places they represent. Many of the maps he has created can be found in books, magazines, videos, Web sites, and public places.

About the Map Illustrator
Matt Kania

On the cover: Do you like to canoe? Enjoy a scenic sunrise at Pleasant Pond.
On page one: It's pumpkin-carving time! Be sure to visit New Hampshire in the fall.

OUR NEW HAMPSHIRE TRIP

New Hampshire's Nickname:
The Granite State

WELCOME
TO NEW
HAMPSHIRE

Let's tour New Hampshire! It's a great place to explore. Just look at all you'll do there.

You'll eat mooseburgers and seafood. You'll watch a star show. You'll see how waterwheels made factories run. You'll rattle up a mountain in a train. You'll meet bears, mountain lions, and moose. You'll pet bunnies and feed baby goats. And you'll watch people making maple syrup!

Just follow that loopy dotted line. Or make your own trip by skipping around. Either way, you're in for a big adventure. So buckle up and hang on tight. We're off to see New Hampshire!

As you travel through New Hampshire, watch for all the interesting facts along the way.

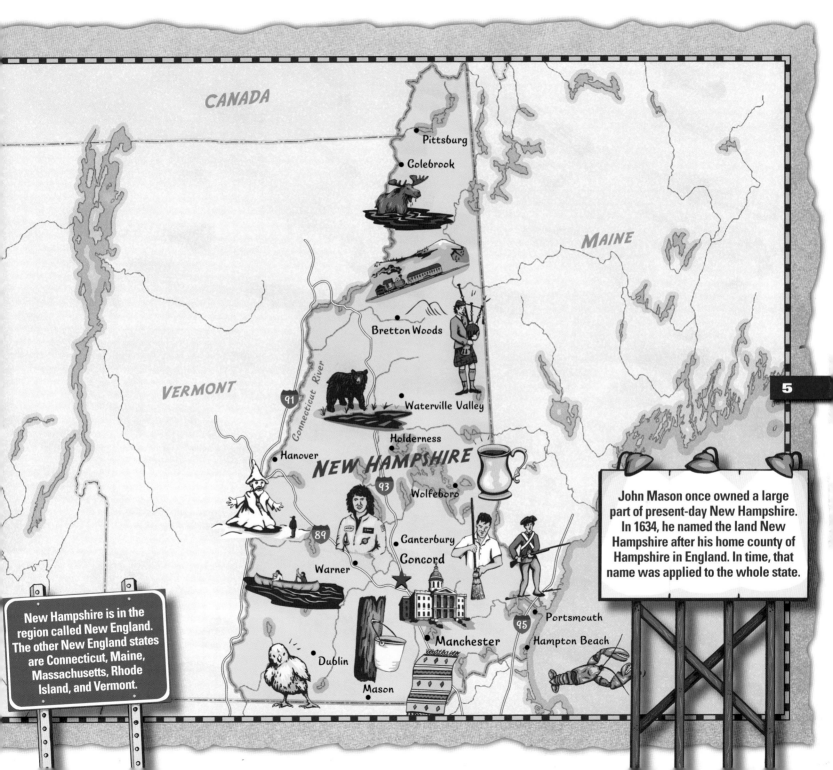

CANADA

MAINE

VERMONT

Pittsburg

Colebrook

Bretton Woods

91

Connecticut River

Waterville Valley

Holderness

Hanover

NEW HAMPSHIRE

93

Wolfeboro

89

Canterbury

Concord

Warner

Manchester

Portsmouth

95

Hampton Beach

Dublin

Mason

John Mason once owned a large part of present-day New Hampshire. In 1634, he named the land New Hampshire after his home county of Hampshire in England. In time, that name was applied to the whole state.

New Hampshire is in the region called New England. The other New England states are Connecticut, Maine, Massachusetts, Rhode Island, and Vermont.

New Hampshire has more than 1,000 lakes. The largest is Lake Winnipesaukee.

New Hampshire's White Mountains offer amazing views! Can you climb to the top?

Mount Washington Observatory and Weather Center is in North Conway. There you'll learn about storms, winds, and other forces of nature.

Looking Out from Mount Washington

Take the little train up Mount Washington. You can get on in Bretton Woods. Mount Washington's slope is really steep! This is New Hampshire's highest peak. It's part of the rugged White Mountains. They cover north-central New Hampshire.

Look north from the mountaintop. You'll see the Great North Woods. Even farther north is Canada!

The Connecticut River rises in the north. It forms most of New Hampshire's western border. Many lakes lie south of the mountains. The Merrimack River runs south from central New Hampshire. Southeastern New Hampshire faces the Atlantic Ocean.

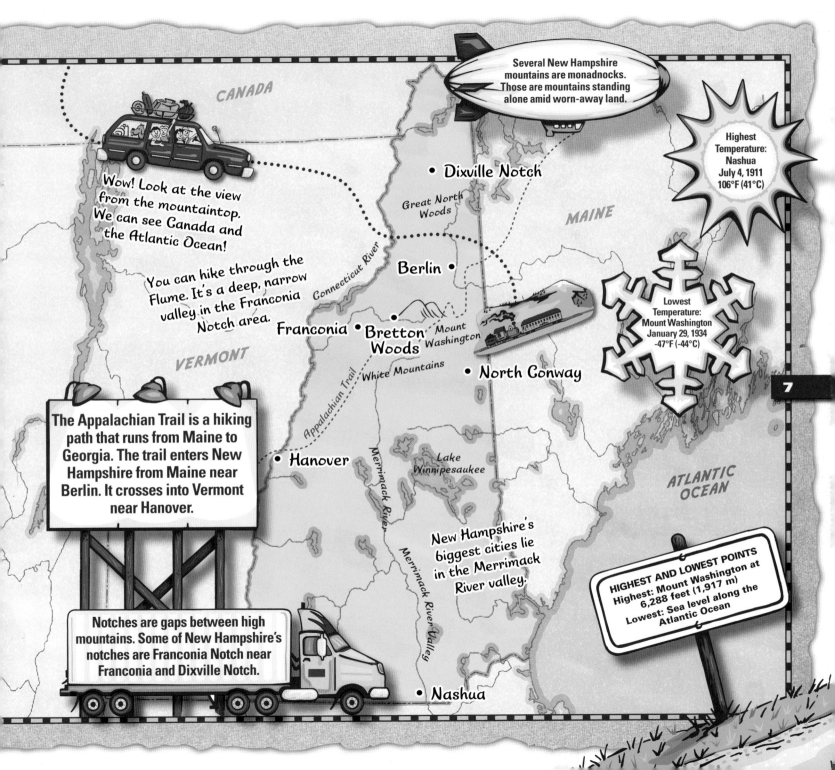

CANADA

Wow! Look at the view from the mountaintop. We can see Canada and the Atlantic Ocean!

You can hike through the Flume. It's a deep, narrow valley in the Franconia Notch area.

Several New Hampshire mountains are monadnocks. Those are mountains standing alone amid worn-away land.

• Dixville Notch

Great North Woods

MAINE

Highest Temperature: Nashua July 4, 1911 106°F (41°C)

Berlin •

Connecticut River

Lowest Temperature: Mount Washington January 29, 1934 -47°F (-44°C)

Franconia • Bretton Woods

Mount Washington

VERMONT

Appalachian Trail

White Mountains

• North Conway

7

The Appalachian Trail is a hiking path that runs from Maine to Georgia. The trail enters New Hampshire from Maine near Berlin. It crosses into Vermont near Hanover.

• Hanover

Merrimack River

Lake Winnipesaukee

ATLANTIC OCEAN

New Hampshire's biggest cities lie in the Merrimack River valley.

Merrimack River Valley

HIGHEST AND LOWEST POINTS
Highest: Mount Washington at 6,288 feet (1,917 m)
Lowest: Sea level along the Atlantic Ocean

Notches are gaps between high mountains. Some of New Hampshire's notches are Franconia Notch near Franconia and Dixville Notch.

• Nashua

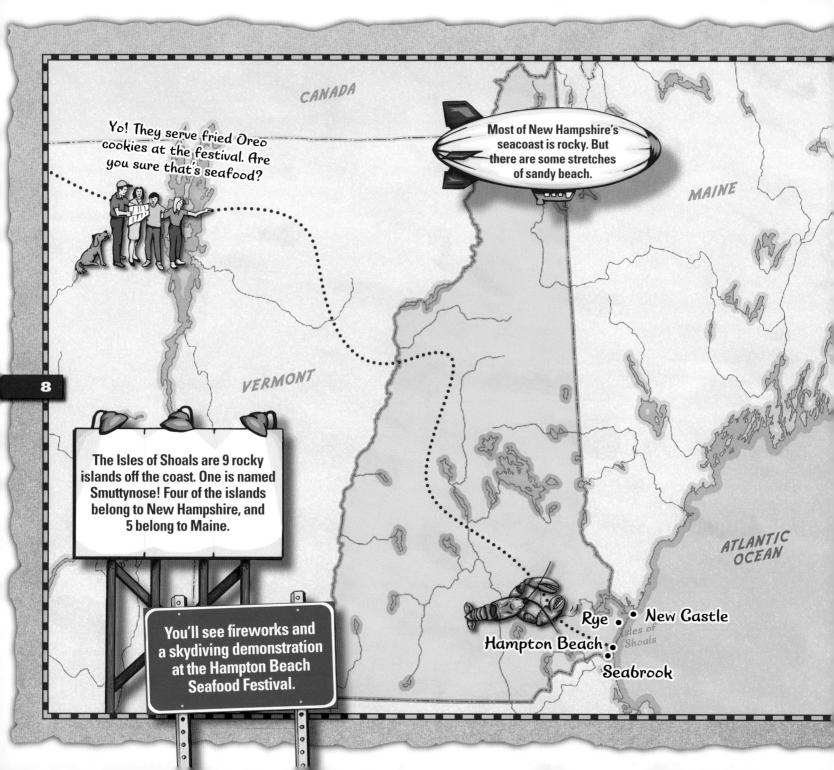

Yo! They serve fried Oreo cookies at the festival. Are you sure that's seafood?

Most of New Hampshire's seacoast is rocky. But there are some stretches of sandy beach.

CANADA

MAINE

VERMONT

The Isles of Shoals are 9 rocky islands off the coast. One is named Smuttynose! Four of the islands belong to New Hampshire, and 5 belong to Maine.

You'll see fireworks and a skydiving demonstration at the Hampton Beach Seafood Festival.

ATLANTIC OCEAN

Rye • • New Castle
Isles of Shoals
Hampton Beach •
Seabrook •

The Hampton Beach Seafood Festival

Chomp on some crunchy grilled shrimp. Snarf down a plate of fried clams. And how would you like your lobster? Broiled, fried, or served in a stew? You're at the Hampton Beach Seafood Festival!

New Hampshire has a short seacoast. It's only 18 miles (29 kilometers) long. But people make the most of it. They enjoy beaches at Rye, New Castle, and Seabrook. Hampton Beach is the most popular spot. It's the perfect place for a seafood festival!

Do you like lobster? Head to the Hampton Beach Seafood Festival!

More than 200,000 people come to the Hampton Beach Seafood Festival every year.

What Are New Hampshire's Fishing Products? Flounder, smelt, lobsters, shrimp, and crabs

This bear calls Squam Lakes Natural Science Center home.

The Seacoast Science Center is in Rye.

Squam Lakes Natural Science Center

Meet the bears. Shh! One might be sleeping. Then check out the mountain lions. Eek! One might jump up right in front of you. You're exploring Squam Lakes Natural Science Center!

This nature center is in Holderness. Wander along its trails. You'll see otters, red foxes, and skunks. They're some of New Hampshire's many wild animals. Don't worry. Glass walls protect you from them.

Forests cover much of the state. Many animals make their homes there. They include deer, beavers, chipmunks, and raccoons. Moose live in the Great North Woods. So do black bears. It's fun to watch them from a safe distance!

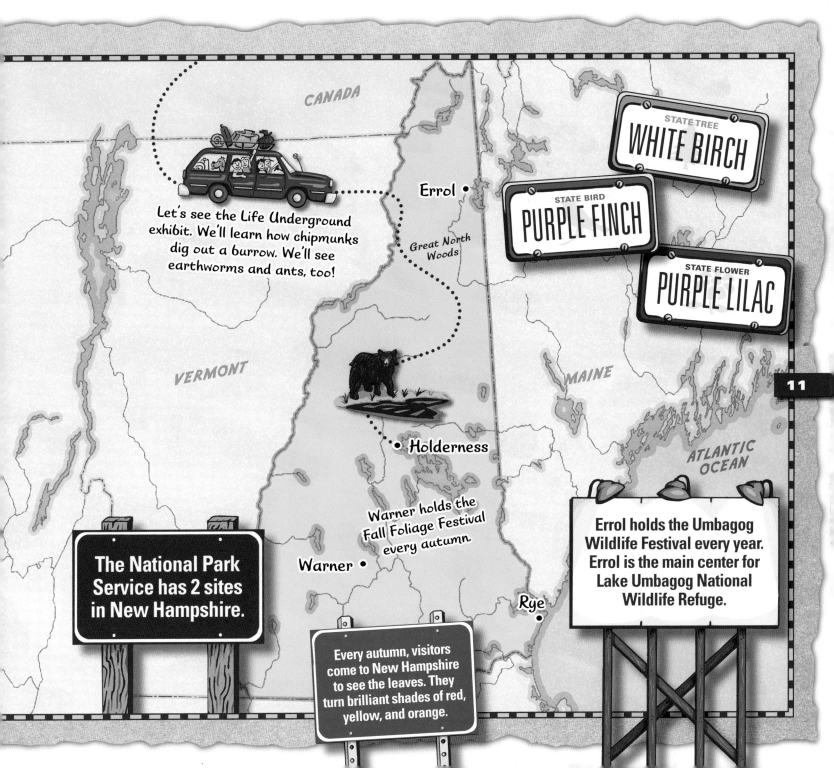

CANADA

Errol

Great North Woods

11

VERMONT

MAINE

ATLANTIC OCEAN

STATE TREE
WHITE BIRCH

STATE BIRD
PURPLE FINCH

STATE FLOWER
PURPLE LILAC

Let's see the Life Underground exhibit. We'll learn how chipmunks dig out a burrow. We'll see earthworms and ants, too!

• Holderness

Warner holds the Fall Foliage Festival every autumn.

Warner •

Rye •

The National Park Service has 2 sites in New Hampshire.

Every autumn, visitors come to New Hampshire to see the leaves. They turn brilliant shades of red, yellow, and orange.

Errol holds the Umbagog Wildlife Festival every year. Errol is the main center for Lake Umbagog National Wildlife Refuge.

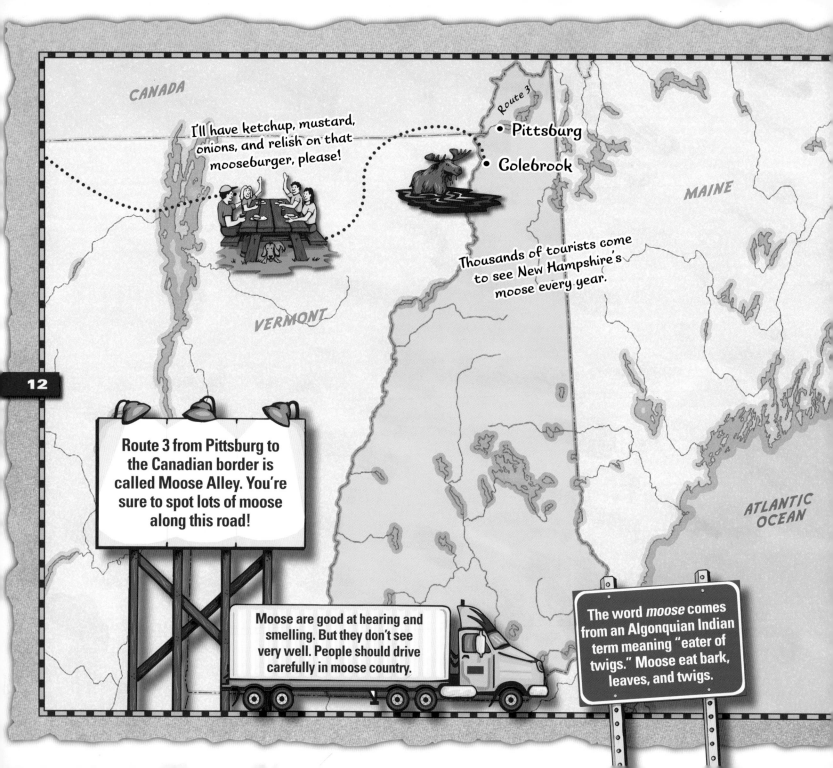

The North Country Moose Festival

Check out this girl's moose hat! She's having fun at the North County Moose Festival.

Want to try a juicy mooseburger? How about some delicious moose stew? You could try the moose-calling contest. Or just take a moose-watching tour. Where can you enjoy all these moose activities? At the North Country Moose Festival!

Big, shaggy moose live in the northern woods. So three towns decided to celebrate them. Colebrook and Pittsburg are two of the towns. The third town is nearby Canaan, Vermont. Together, they hold the moose festival every year!

Want to see lots of moose? Then travel along Moose Alley. It runs north from Pittsburg. Happy moose-watching!

Moose are one of the largest land animals in North America.

New Hampshire was part of the Massachusetts Bay Colony from 1641 to 1680.

Mount Kearsarge Indian Museum in Warner

Wander through Mount Kearsarge Indian Museum. You'll learn all about various Native American **cultures.** You'll see canoes, pottery, and religious objects.

Then follow the path through the Medicine Woods. Signs tell how Native Americans used various plants. They used them for medicines, foods, and dyes.

Many Indian groups once lived in New Hampshire. They built homes with bark and animal skins. They hunted, fished, and farmed. Englishman David Thomson arrived in 1623. He settled at Odiorne Point in what is now Rye. That was New Hampshire's first European settlement. New Hampshire became an English **colony.**

14

Want to learn about Native American culture? Visit Mount Kearsarge Indian Museum!

The towns of Exeter and Hampton were founded in 1638.

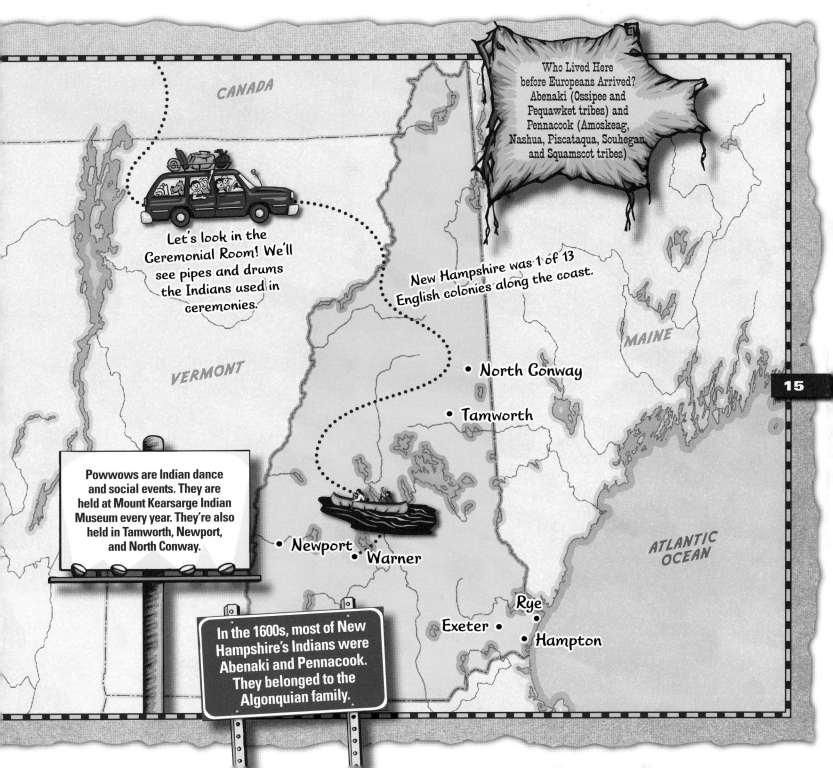

Let's look in the Ceremonial Room! We'll see pipes and drums the Indians used in ceremonies.

Who Lived Here before Europeans Arrived? Abenaki (Ossipee and Pequawket tribes) and Pennacook (Amoskeag, Nashua, Piscataqua, Souhegan and Squamscot tribes)

New Hampshire was 1 of 13 English colonies along the coast.

CANADA

VERMONT

MAINE

• North Conway

• Tamworth

Powwows are Indian dance and social events. They are held at Mount Kearsarge Indian Museum every year. They're also held in Tamworth, Newport, and North Conway.

• Newport • Warner

ATLANTIC OCEAN

Rye
Exeter •
• Hampton

In the 1600s, most of New Hampshire's Indians were Abenaki and Pennacook. They belonged to the Algonquian family.

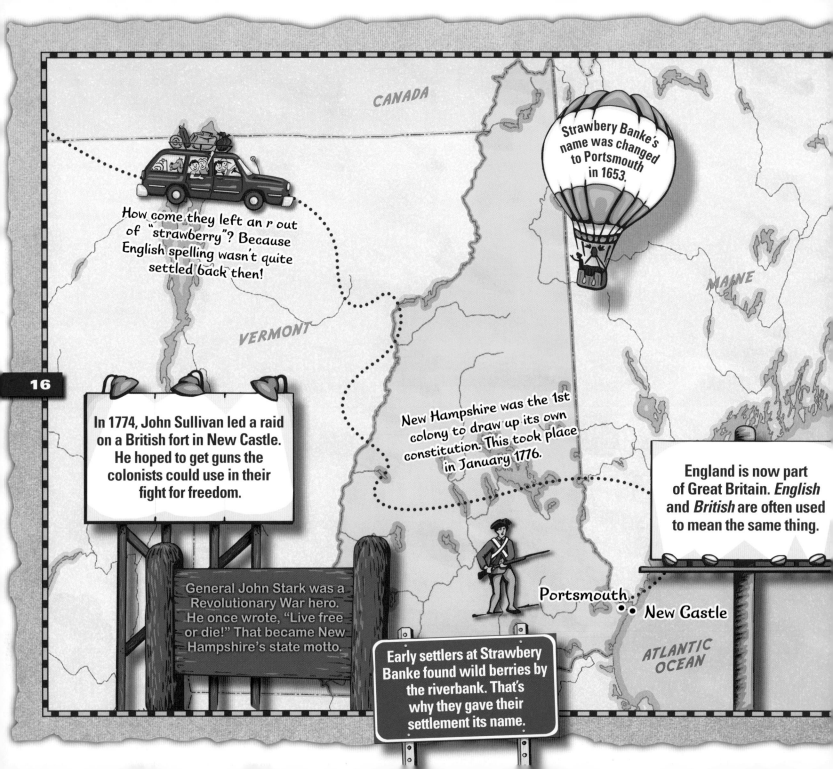

Strawbery Banke's name was changed to Portsmouth in 1653.

How come they left an r out of "strawberry"? Because English spelling wasn't quite settled back then!

CANADA

VERMONT

MAINE

In 1774, John Sullivan led a raid on a British fort in New Castle. He hoped to get guns the colonists could use in their fight for freedom.

New Hampshire was the 1st colony to draw up its own constitution. This took place in January 1776.

England is now part of Great Britain. *English* and *British* are often used to mean the same thing.

General John Stark was a Revolutionary War hero. He once wrote, "Live free or die!" That became New Hampshire's state motto.

Portsmouth

New Castle

ATLANTIC OCEAN

Early settlers at Strawbery Banke found wild berries by the riverbank. That's why they gave their settlement its name.

Strawbery Banke in Portsmouth

Stroll down the sunny lanes. Craftspeople are busy with their trades. You can try out some crafts yourself. Or play kids' games from the 1600s. You're visiting Strawbery Banke!

English colonists settled at Strawbery Banke in 1630. It grew into the busy seaport city of Portsmouth.

In time, the colonists became restless. Great Britain charged high taxes and controlled trade. New Hampshire decided to form its own government. It drew up its own **constitution.**

Colonists fought for freedom in the Revolutionary War (1775–1783). And they won! The colonies became the United States of America.

What was life like in the 1600s? Tour Strawbery Banke and find out!

New Hampshire was the 9th state to enter the Union. It joined on June 21, 1788.

Would you have made a good millworker?
Find out at the Millyard Museum.

You can tour Littleton Grist Mill in Littleton. It's on the Ammonoosuc River. This mill ground grain into flour.

Manchester's Millyard Museum

Explore the Millyard Museum. You'll learn how New Hampshire's early factories worked. This site was once a cotton mill. It stood beside the Merrimack River. The river's water turned a huge waterwheel. The wheel ran the mill's machines. They turned cotton into cloth.

New Hampshire's **industries** grew in the 1850s. Many mills and factories were built. Some made cotton or wool cloth. Others made boots and shoes. Sawmills made lumber and other wood products. Portsmouth became an important shipbuilding center, too.

Manchester became the state's biggest manufacturing center. Many **immigrants** came to work in the mills. Even children worked long hours there.

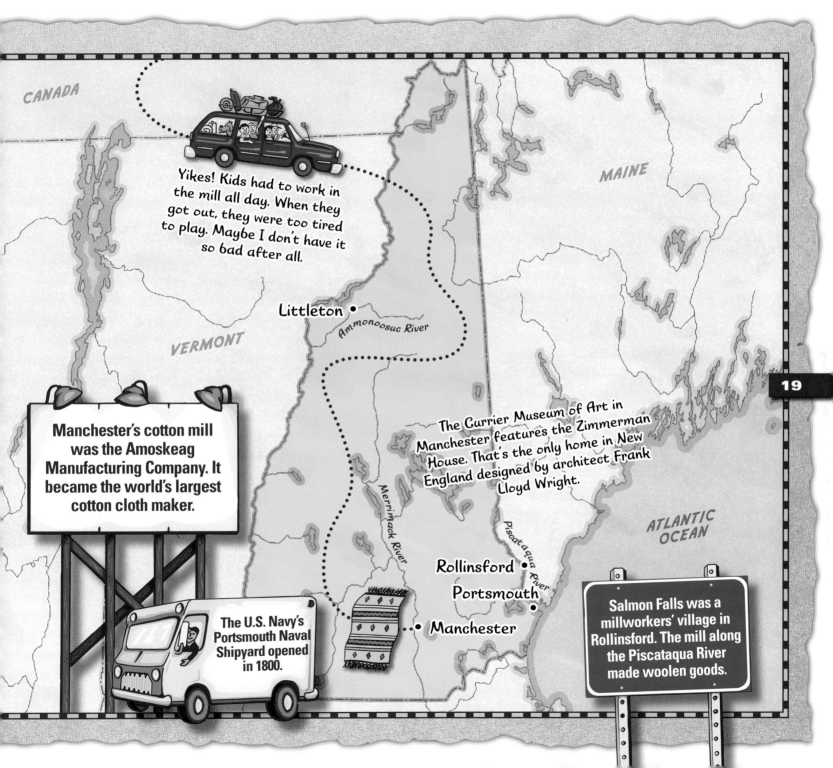

CANADA

MAINE

VERMONT

Yikes! Kids had to work in the mill all day. When they got out, they were too tired to play. Maybe I don't have it so bad after all.

Littleton •

Ammonoosuc River

The Currier Museum of Art in Manchester features the Zimmerman House. That's the only home in New England designed by architect Frank Lloyd Wright.

ATLANTIC OCEAN

Manchester's cotton mill was the Amoskeag Manufacturing Company. It became the world's largest cotton cloth maker.

Merrimack River

Piscataqua River

Rollinsford •

Portsmouth •

• Manchester

The U.S. Navy's Portsmouth Naval Shipyard opened in 1800.

Salmon Falls was a millworkers' village in Rollinsford. The mill along the Piscataqua River made woolen goods.

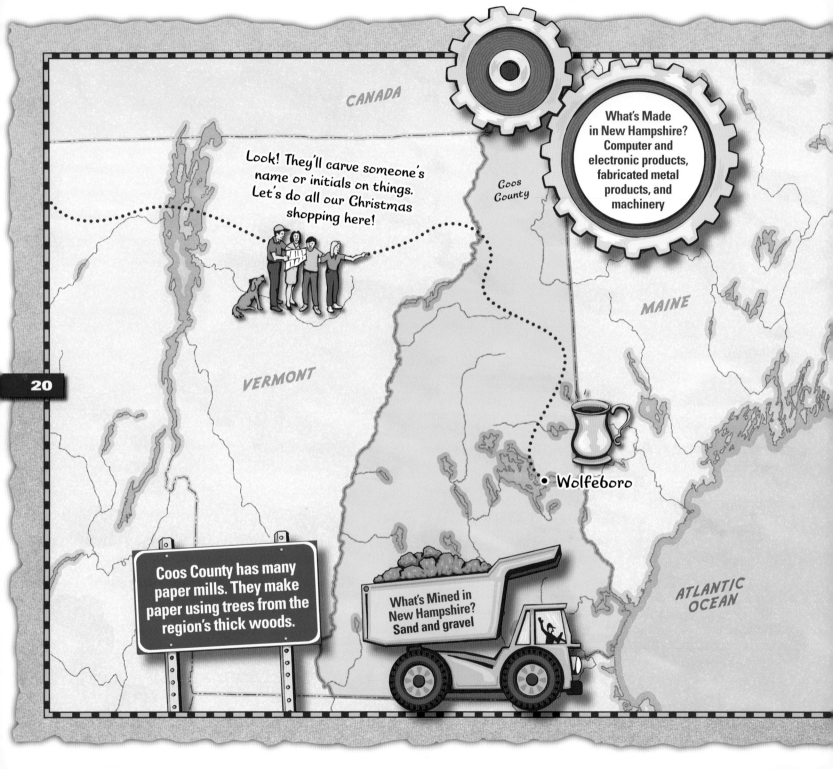

CANADA

Look! They'll carve someone's name or initials on things. Let's do all our Christmas shopping here!

Coos County

What's Made in New Hampshire? Computer and electronic products, fabricated metal products, and machinery

MAINE

VERMONT

Wolfeboro

Coos County has many paper mills. They make paper using trees from the region's thick woods.

What's Mined in New Hampshire? Sand and gravel

ATLANTIC OCEAN

Hampshire Pewter in Wolfeboro

Want to see amazing craftspeople at work? Head to Hampshire Pewter!

Most factories use machines to make things. But Hampshire Pewter makes things the old-fashioned way. Skilled craftspeople are hard at work there. And you can watch them!

First, workers mix tin with other metals. This produces pewter. Then they pour the melted metal into molds. Molds might be shaped like mugs, cups, or spoons. The gray metal hardens as it cools. Finally, the workers polish each piece.

New Hampshire had some of the nation's earliest factories. The state has grown with the times, though. Computer products are its major factory goods now!

How do those dancers remember all those steps? It takes a lot of practice!

Waterville Valley's Celtic Festival

Irish step dancers prance across a stage. Harpists and bagpipers play **traditional** tunes. People push smooth stones across the ice. They're competing in an ancient game called curling. Sheepdogs compete in a contest, too. They show how well they round up sheep!

You're enjoying the Celtic Festival. It celebrates Irish and Scottish culture.

New Hampshire welcomed many Irish and Scottish immigrants. Others came from England, Wales, Germany, and Italy. French Canadians arrived from Canada, too. Many immigrants worked in the mills. Others opened shops or worked on farms.

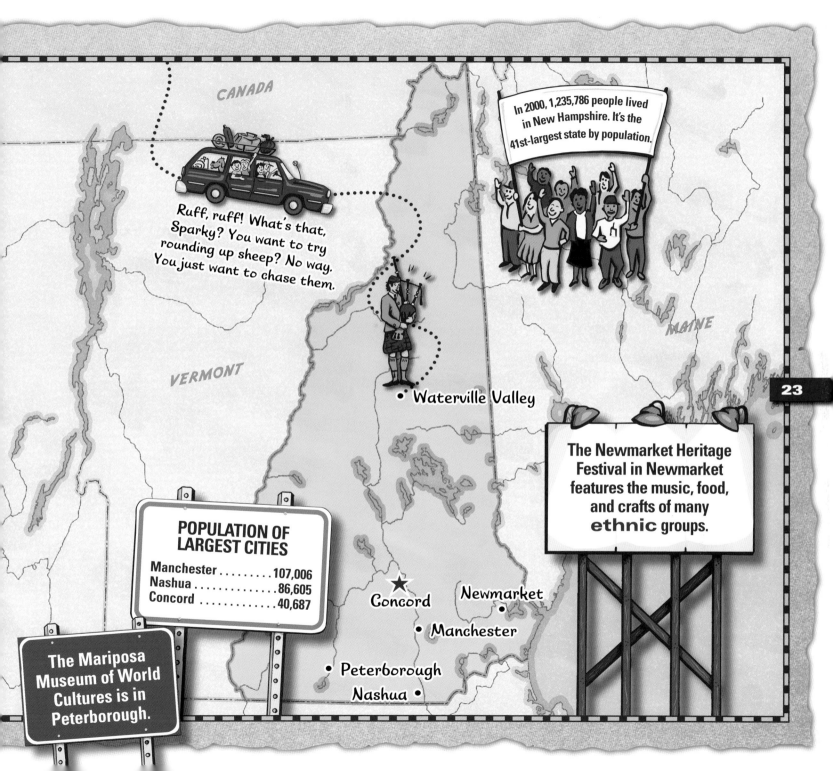

CANADA

Ruff, ruff! What's that, Sparky? You want to try rounding up sheep? No way. You just want to chase them.

In 2000, 1,235,786 people lived in New Hampshire. It's the 41st-largest state by population.

MAINE

VERMONT

23

• Waterville Valley

The Newmarket Heritage Festival in Newmarket features the music, food, and crafts of many **ethnic** groups.

POPULATION OF LARGEST CITIES

Manchester 107,006
Nashua 86,605
Concord 40,687

★ Concord

Newmarket
•

• Manchester

The Mariposa Museum of World Cultures is in Peterborough.

• Peterborough

Nashua •

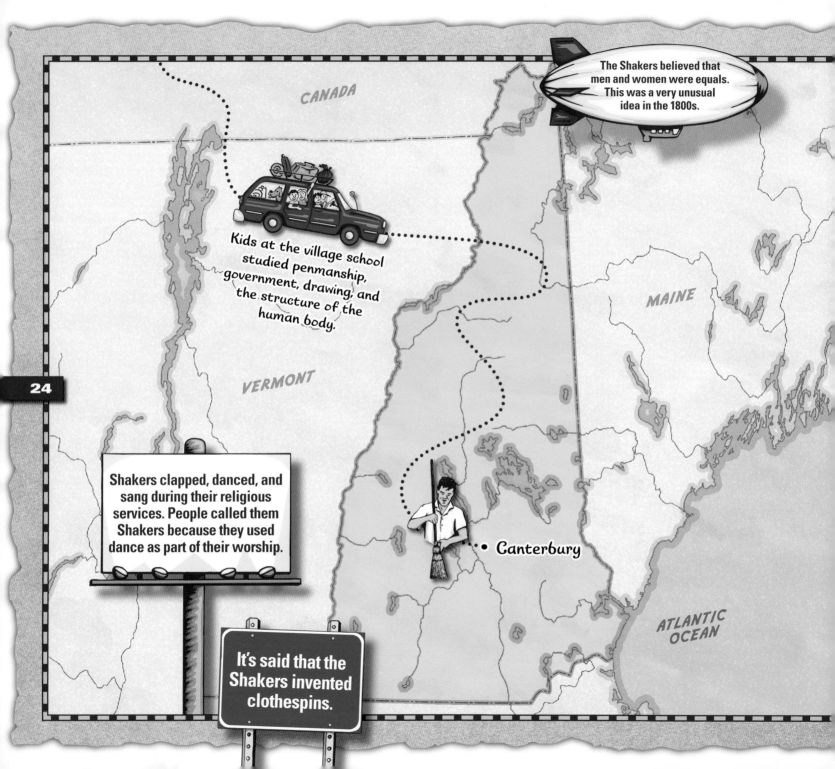

CANADA

The Shakers believed that men and women were equals. This was a very unusual idea in the 1800s.

Kids at the village school studied penmanship, government, drawing, and the structure of the human body.

MAINE

VERMONT

Shakers clapped, danced, and sang during their religious services. People called them Shakers because they used dance as part of their worship.

• Canterbury

ATLANTIC OCEAN

It's said that the Shakers invented clothespins.

Canterbury Shaker Village

New Hampshire's factories were buzzing with activity in the 1800s. But farms were thriving, too. Want a glimpse of farm life back then? Just visit Canterbury Shaker Village!

The Shakers were a religious group. They lived a simple farming life. All land and buildings belonged to the whole community. Everyone worked hard for the good of all.

You'll see many Shaker activities in the village. Some people are making brooms and boxes. Spinners and weavers are making clothes. You'll see the bee house and horse barn. In the bakery, check out the wood-burning oven. It baked sixty loaves of bread at once!

Don't forget to visit Canterbury Shaker Village. You'll see Shaker craftspeople at work.

Canterbury was established in 1792. By the 1850s, 300 people lived in the village.

Cheep, cheep! Check out the chicks at the Friendly Farm!

Contoocook holds the Sheep and Wool Festival every year.

Hold a fluffy chick. Feed a baby goat. Oink with the pigs. Or cuddle a fleecy lamb. You're visiting the Friendly Farm in Dublin!

You'll get friendly with the farm animals here. The farmers are friendly, too. They hope you'll love farming as they do!

Many New Hampshire farmers raise dairy cows. Their milk is made into butter and ice cream. Hay is the major field crop. It's used as animal feed. Apples are important crops, too. The top farm products are not foods, though. They're plants for people's homes. That includes Christmas trees!

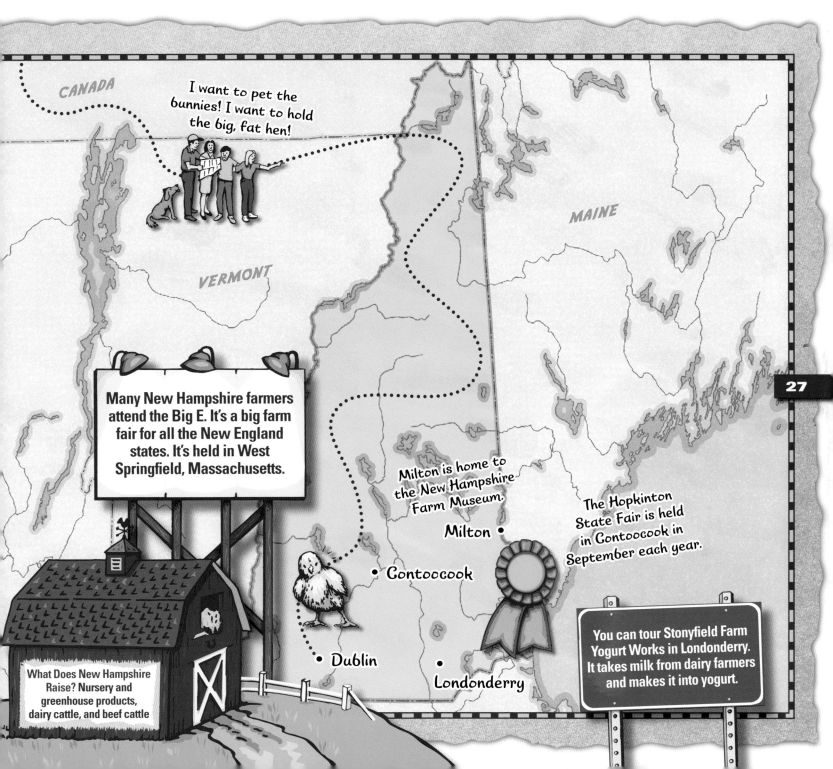

I want to pet the bunnies! I want to hold the big, fat hen!

CANADA

MAINE

VERMONT

Many New Hampshire farmers attend the Big E. It's a big farm fair for all the New England states. It's held in West Springfield, Massachusetts.

Milton is home to the New Hampshire Farm Museum.

Milton •

The Hopkinton State Fair is held in Contoocook in September each year.

• Contoocook

What Does New Hampshire Raise? Nursery and greenhouse products, dairy cattle, and beef cattle

• Dublin

• Londonderry

You can tour Stonyfield Farm Yogurt Works in Londonderry. It takes milk from dairy farmers and makes it into yogurt.

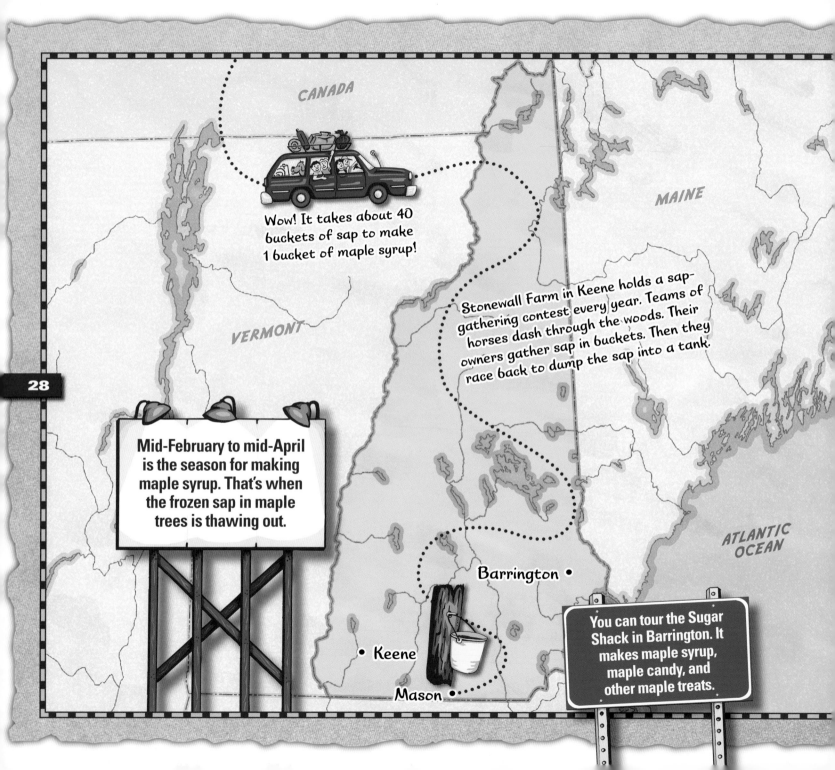

CANADA

MAINE

VERMONT

Wow! It takes about 40 buckets of sap to make 1 bucket of maple syrup!

Stonewall Farm in Keene holds a sap-gathering contest every year. Teams of horses dash through the woods. Their owners gather sap in buckets. Then they race back to dump the sap into a tank.

Mid-February to mid-April is the season for making maple syrup. That's when the frozen sap in maple trees is thawing out.

ATLANTIC OCEAN

Barrington •

You can tour the Sugar Shack in Barrington. It makes maple syrup, maple candy, and other maple treats.

• Keene

Mason •

Parker's Maple Barn in Mason

Is it early spring? Do you smell something sweet in the air? You must be near a sugarhouse! That's where people make maple syrup.

Many New Hampshire sugarhouses give tours. One is Parker's Maple Barn. There you'll learn all about making maple syrup.

You'll see how **sap** is collected from maple trees. You'll also learn how Indians made maple sugar. They put hot rocks into the sap! Next, you'll see a blazing wood fire. Over it, the sap is boiling in big tanks. Finally, the finished syrup is poured into jugs. Is your mouth watering yet?

Yum, maple syrup! See how it's made at Parker's Maple Barn.

New Hampshire produces about 90,000 gallons (340,700 L) of maple syrup every year!

Franklin Pierce was the 14th president (1853–1857). He was born in Hillsboro.

The State Capitol in Concord

Daniel Webster was a New Hampshire politician. His statue stands outside New Hampshire's capitol.

What's the capitol made of? Granite, of course! New Hampshire is called the Granite State. It has huge deposits of this building stone. Granite is strong and solid. It's beautiful, too!

It's a good thing the capitol is solid. It houses the state government offices. New Hampshire's government has three branches. One branch makes the state's laws. It's called the General Court. Another branch makes sure laws are obeyed. This branch is headed by the governor. Judges make up the third branch. They decide whether someone has broken the law.

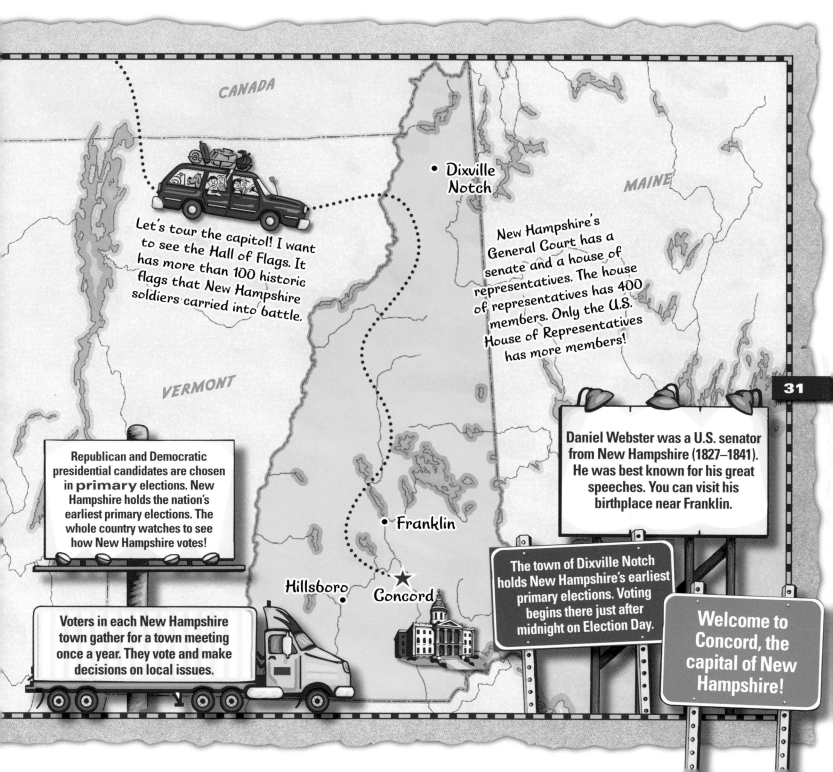

Let's tour the capitol! I want to see the Hall of Flags. It has more than 100 historic flags that New Hampshire soldiers carried into battle.

New Hampshire's General Court has a senate and a house of representatives. The house of representatives has 400 members. Only the U.S. House of Representatives has more members!

Daniel Webster was a U.S. senator from New Hampshire (1827–1841). He was best known for his great speeches. You can visit his birthplace near Franklin.

Republican and Democratic presidential candidates are chosen in **primary** elections. New Hampshire holds the nation's earliest primary elections. The whole country watches to see how New Hampshire votes!

The town of Dixville Notch holds New Hampshire's earliest primary elections. Voting begins there just after midnight on Election Day.

Voters in each New Hampshire town gather for a town meeting once a year. They vote and make decisions on local issues.

Welcome to Concord, the capital of New Hampshire!

CANADA

MAINE

VERMONT

• Dixville Notch

• Franklin

Hillsboro •

★ Concord

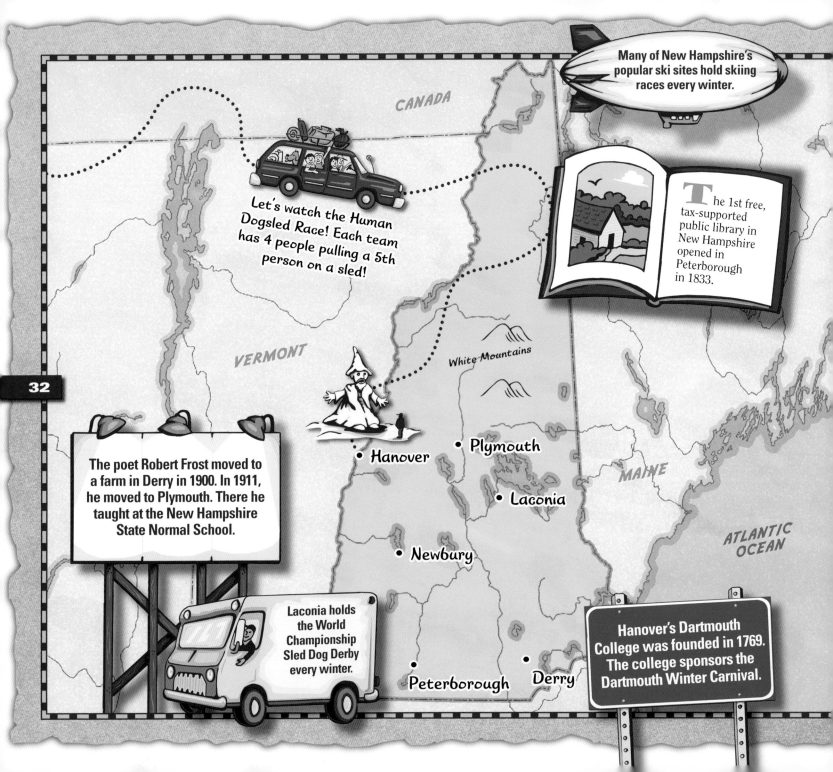

Many of New Hampshire's popular ski sites hold skiing races every winter.

The 1st free, tax-supported public library in New Hampshire opened in Peterborough in 1833.

Let's watch the Human Dogsled Race! Each team has 4 people pulling a 5th person on a sled!

CANADA

VERMONT

White Mountains

Plymouth

Hanover

Laconia

MAINE

The poet Robert Frost moved to a farm in Derry in 1900. In 1911, he moved to Plymouth. There he taught at the New Hampshire State Normal School.

Newbury

ATLANTIC OCEAN

Laconia holds the World Championship Sled Dog Derby every winter.

Peterborough

Derry

Hanover's Dartmouth College was founded in 1769. The college sponsors the Dartmouth Winter Carnival.

The Dartmouth Winter Carnival in Hanover

Gaze at the ice sculptures. Most are bigger than you! Then check out the polar bear swim. You won't spot any polar bears, though. You'll see people who aren't wearing very much. They jump into icy water for a swim!

This is the Dartmouth Winter Carnival. It's one of New Hampshire's many winter festivals. Winter also brings in thousands of skiers. They ski the snowy slopes of the White Mountains.

There's plenty to do when it's warmer, too. Some people enjoy the seaside beaches. And some just drive around. They admire the little villages and the colorful leaves.

It's the Cat in the Hat! The Dartmouth Winter Carnival features amazing ice sculptures.

The League of New Hampshire Craftsmen's Fair takes place at Mount Sunapee Resort in Newbury.

Feel like learning about the stars? Head to the Christa McAuliffe Planetarium.

34

Concord's Christa McAuliffe Planetarium

Lean back and watch the night sky unfold. Which objects are stars? Which are planets? What patterns do the stars make? You'll learn all this and more. You're at the Christa McAuliffe Planetarium. And you're watching an exciting sky show!

Who was Christa McAuliffe? She was a schoolteacher in Concord. She was chosen to fly aboard the space shuttle *Challenger*. Concord and the whole state were excited. Sadly, the shuttle exploded after takeoff. Everyone aboard was killed.

Christa McAuliffe loved teaching kids. This planetarium was built in her honor. It's a great place to carry on her work!

Alan Shepard became the 1st U.S. astronaut in space in 1961. He was born in East Derry.

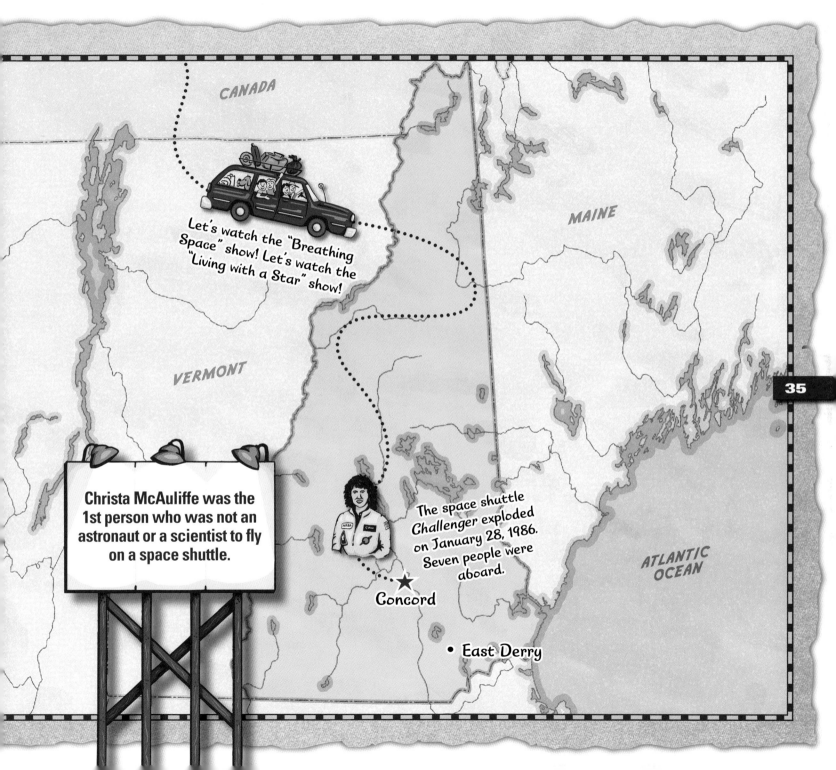

CANADA

MAINE

VERMONT

Let's watch the "Breathing Space" show! Let's watch the "Living with a Star" show!

Christa McAuliffe was the 1st person who was not an astronaut or a scientist to fly on a space shuttle.

The space shuttle *Challenger* exploded on January 28, 1986. Seven people were aboard.

ATLANTIC OCEAN

★ Concord

• East Derry

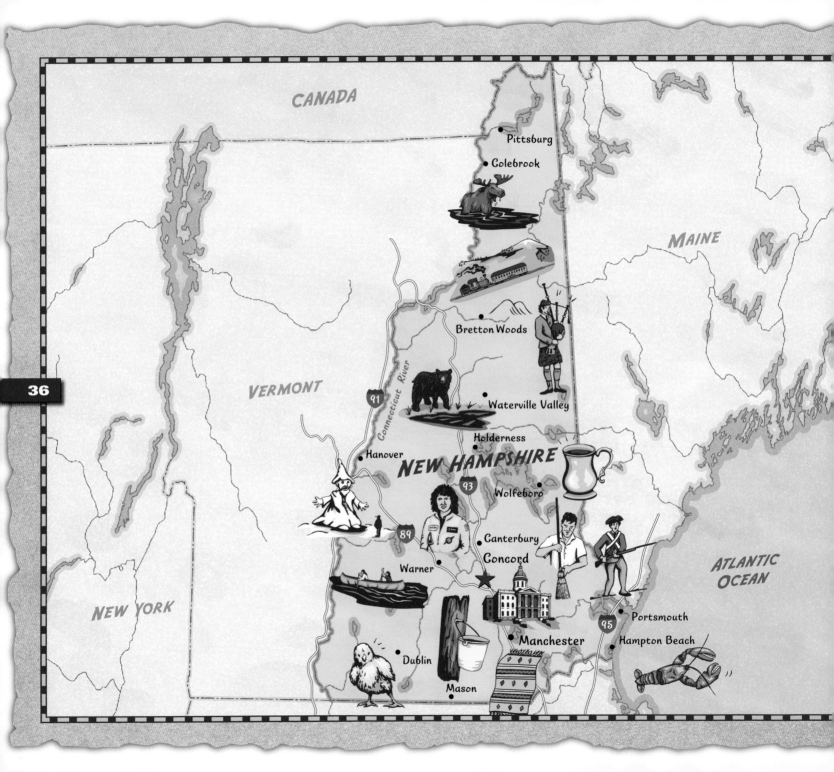

CANADA

Pittsburg

Colebrook

MAINE

VERMONT

Bretton Woods

Connecticut River

Waterville Valley

Holderness

NEW HAMPSHIRE

Hanover

Wolfeboro

91

93

89

Canterbury

Concord

Warner

ATLANTIC OCEAN

NEW YORK

Portsmouth

95

Hampton Beach

Dublin

Manchester

Mason

OUR TRIP

We visited many amazing places on our trip! We also met a lot of interesting people along the way. Look at the map on the left. Use your finger to trace all the places we have been.

Who originally gave New Hampshire its name? See page 5 for the answer.

What is the largest lake in New Hampshire? Page 6 has the answer.

How many islands make up the Isles of Shoals? See page 8 for the answer.

Where is Moose Alley? Look on page 12 for the answer.

What are powwows? Page 15 has the answer.

How did Strawbery Banke get its name? Turn to page 16 for the answer.

What kind of mills can you find in Coos County? Look on page 20 for the answer.

What town holds the World Championship Sled Dog Derby? Turn to page 32 for the answer.

That was a great trip! We have traveled all over New Hampshire!
There are a few places that we didn't have time for, though. Next time, we plan to visit the Children's Museum of Portsmouth. Visitors enjoy a variety of activities, including digging for fossils and playing African drums. If we have time, we can even take a trolley ride!

More Places to Visit in New Hampshire

WORDS TO KNOW

colony (KOL-uh-nee) a land with ties to a parent country

constitution (kon-stuh-TOO-shuhn) a statement of the basic laws and ideas that govern a state or nation

culture (KUHL-chur) a group of people's beliefs, customs, and way of life

ethnic (ETH-nik) relating to a person's race or nationality

immigrants (IM-uh-gruhnts) people who move to another country

industries (IN-duh-streez) types of businesses

primary (PRYE-mair-ee) 1st or earliest

sap (SAP) the liquid that circulates within a plant

traditional (truh-DISH-uh-nuhl) following long-held customs

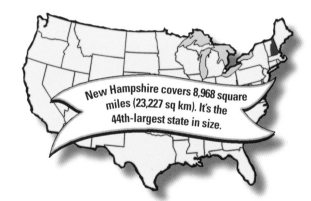

New Hampshire covers 8,968 square miles (23,227 sq km). It's the 44th-largest state in size.

STATE SYMBOLS

State amphibian: Spotted newt

State animal: White-tailed deer

State bird: Purple finch

State butterfly: Karner blue

State flower: Purple lilac

State freshwater fish: Brook trout

State insect: Ladybug

State mineral: Beryl

State rock: Granite

State saltwater fish: Striped bass

State sport: Skiing

State tree: White birch

State wildflower: Pink lady's slipper

State flag

State seal

STATE SONGS

"Old New Hampshire"

Words by Dr. John F. Holmes, music by Maurice Hoffmann

With a skill that knows no measure,
From the golden store of Fate
God, in His great love and wisdom,
Made the rugged Granite State;
Made the lakes, the fields, the forests;
Made the Rivers and the rills;
Made the bubbling, crystal fountains
Of New Hampshire's Granite Hills.

Chorus:
Old New Hampshire, Old New Hampshire
Old New Hampshire Grand and Great
We will sing of Old New Hampshire,
Of the dear old Granite State.

Built he New Hampshire glorious
From the borders to the sea;
And with matchless charm and splendor
Blessed her for eternity.
Hers, the majesty of mountain;
Hers, the grandeur of the lake;
Hers, the truth as from the hillside
Whence her crystal waters break.

(Chorus)

FAMOUS PEOPLE

Beach, Amy Marcy Cheney (1867–1944), pianist and composer

Brown, Alice (1856–1948), author

Burns, Ken (1953–), documentary filmmaker

Chase, Salmon P. (1808–1873), politician and jurist

Cochran, Barbara (1951–), Olympic skier

Eddy, Mary Baker (1821–1910), founder of the Christian Science Church

Fisk, Carlton (1947–), baseball player

Flynn, Elizabeth Gurley (1890–1964), founding member of the American Civil Liberties Union

Frost, Robert (1874–1963), poet

Greeley, Horace (1811–1872), journalist and political leader

Irving, John (1942–), author

Jacobi, Lotte (1896–1990), photographer

McAuliffe, Christa (1948–1986), astronaut

Montana, Bob (1920–1975), cartoonist

Pierce, Franklin (1804–1869), 14th U.S. president

Porter, Eleanor (1868–1920), children's author

Salinger, J. D. (1919–), author

Shepard, Alan, Jr. (1923–1998), astronaut

Tupper, Earl (1907–1983), inventor of Tupperware

Webster, Daniel (1782–1852), lawyer and statesman

TO FIND OUT MORE

At the Library

Ferry, Steven. *Franklin Pierce: Our Fourteenth President*. Chanhassen, Minn.: The Child's World, 2002.

Fradin, Dennis B. *New Hampshire*. Chicago: Children's Press, 1992.

Hall, Donald, and Michael McCurdy (illustrator). *Lucy's Summer*. San Diego: Harcourt Brace, 1995.

Harris, Marie, and Karen Busch Holman (illustrator). *Primary Numbers: A New Hampshire Number Book*. Chelsea, Mich.: Sleeping Bear Press, 2004.

On the Web

Visit our home page for lots of links about New Hampshire:
http://www.childsworld.com/links

Note to Parents, Teachers, and Librarians: We routinely verify our Web links to make sure they are safe, active sites—so encourage your readers to check them out!

Places to Visit or Contact

Museum of New Hampshire History
The Hamel Center
6 Eagle Square
Concord, NH 03301
603/228-6688
For more information about the history of New Hampshire

New Hampshire Division of Travel and Tourism Development
172 Pembroke Road
PO Box 1856
Concord, NH 03302
603/271-2665
For more information about traveling in New Hampshire

INDEX

Bye, Granite State.
We had a great time.
We'll come back soon!